BILBO'S LAST SONG

J.R.R. Tolkien

Illustrated by Pauline Baynes

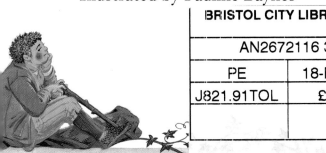

HUTCHINSON

London Sydney Auckland Johannesburg

Bilbo's Last Song
A HUTCHINSON BOOK 0 09 188488 8

First published in Great Britain by Unwin Hyman Ltd 1990

This edition published by Hutchinson 2002
A division of The Random House Group Ltd

1 3 5 7 9 10 8 6 4 2

Text © The Order of the Holy Paraclete, 1974
Illustrations © Pauline Baynes, 1990

The right of J.R.R. Tolkien and Pauline Baynes to be identified as the
author and illustrator of this work has been asserted in accordance with the
Copyright, Designs and Patents Act 1988.

The quotations are taken from the second hardback edition of *The Lord of the Rings* (© George Allen &
Unwin (Publishers) Ltd, 1966) and the fourth hardback edition of *The Hobbit* (© George Allen & Unwin
(Publishers) Ltd 1978) and are reproduced by kind permission of HarperCollins*Publishers*.

RANDOM HOUSE CHILDREN'S BOOKS
61-63 Uxbridge Rd, London W5 5SA
RANDOM HOUSE AUSTRALIA (PTY) LTD
20 Alfred Street, Milsons Point, Sydney, New South Wales 2061, Australia
RANDOM HOUSE NEW ZEALAND LTD
18 Poland Road, Glenfield, Auckland 10, New Zealand
RANDOM HOUSE (PTY) LTD
Endulini, 5A Jubilee Road, Parktown 2193, South Africa

THE RANDOM HOUSE GROUP Limited Reg. No. 954009
www.**kids**at**randomhouse**.co.uk

A CIP catalogue record for this book is available from the British Library.

Printed in Singapore by Tien Wah Press [PTE]

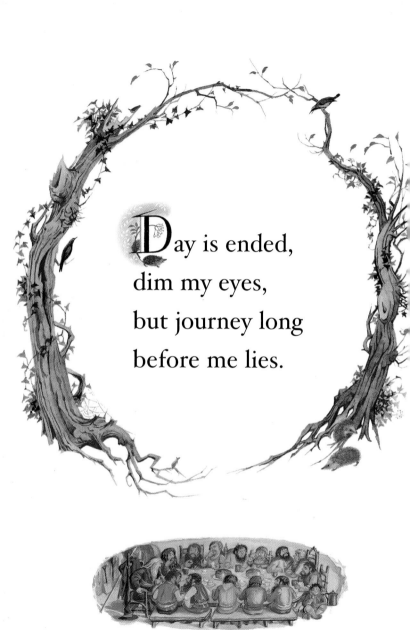

Day is ended,
dim my eyes,
but journey long
before me lies.

Farewell, friends!
I hear the call.
The ship's beside
the stony wall.

Foam is white
and waves are grey;
beyond the sunset
leads my way.

Foam is salt,
the wind is free;
I hear the rising
of the Sea.

Farewell, friends!
The sails are set,
the wind is east,
the moorings fret.

Shadows long
before me lie,
beneath the
ever-bending sky,

But islands lie
behind the Sun
that I shall raise
ere all is done;

Lands there are
to west of West,
where night is quiet
and sleep is rest.

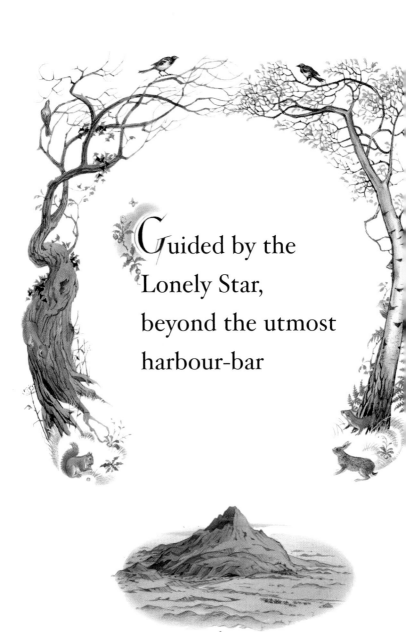

Guided by the
Lonely Star,
beyond the utmost
harbour-bar

I'll find the havens
fair and free,
and beaches of
the Starlit Sea.

Ship, my ship!
I seek the West,
and fields
and mountains
ever blest.

Farewell to Middle-earth at last,
I see the Star above your mast!

NOTES ON THE PICTURES

The pictures in this book spring from two sources. The large paintings on the right-hand pages are based on episodes at the end of *The Lord of the Rin* (the specific volume is referred to by its initials), in which the Ring-bearers ride westwards to the Grey Havens, where they take ship for the Undying Lands. The narrative describes Frodo and Sam riding to meet a company including Bilbo, Elrond, Galadriel and Gildor, as well as many other elves. We may assume that this party had set out from Rivendell: Elrond had told Frodo two years before that he would soon depart. (ROTK, p. 267)

The poem that forms the text of this book is Bilbo's. Like Elrond, he ha indicated to Frodo that his thoughts were turning towards departure. (ROTK, p. 266)

It therefore seemed right to think of the beginning of that last journey, and of Bilbo's part in it. The first four large pictures are thus based on a sequence of events which we can only imagine, but which must logically ha occurred.

The smaller pictures, running at the bottom of both left- and right-han pages, show scenes from *The Hobbit*. Bilbo (portrayed at the left-hand side c the page) remembers his first journey as he goes on his last journey.

Endpapers. 'None saw them pass, save the wild creatures.' (ROTK, p. 310 The picture shows the 'many Elves of the High Kindred' who accompanied Elrond, Galadriel, Gildor and Bilbo on their last journey through the autumnal countryside. Galadriel leads the procession, riding a white palfrey, followed by Gildor. Elrond rides behind Gildor, and is partly masked by the tree in the centre. Bilbo on his grey pony appears on the left-hand page, in the foreground.

1. There are several fleeting glimpses of Bilbo at Rivendell 'in his little roon It was littered with papers and pens and pencils'. (ROTK, p. 264)

i. 'A perfectly round door like a porthole, painted green, with a shiny yellow brass knob in the exact middle.' (H, p. 11)

'All that the unsuspecting Bilbo saw that morning was an old man with a [st]aff.' (H, p. 13)

Bilbo looking out of his window, thinking about making his last journey. [T]he window opened on to the gardens and looked south across the ravine of [th]e Bruinen.' (FOTR, p. 250)

'Gandalf sat at the head of the party with the thirteen dwarves all round: [an]d Bilbo sat on a stool at the fireside.' (H, p. 19)

After his unexpected tea-party, Bilbo slept late the following morning. In [co]nsequence, he didn't get the dwarves' letter until half past ten – and had [te]n minutes to meet them at eleven o'clock at the Green Dragon Inn, [By]water. 'Bilbo could never remember how he found himself outside . . . [ru]nning as fast as his furry feet could carry him.' (H, p. 33)

It was just as Frodo and the other hobbits left Rivendell to return to the [Sh]ire on 5th October 3019 (Shire Reckoning 1419) that Elrond said, 'About [th]is time of year, when the leaves are gold before they fall, look for Bilbo in [th]e woods of the Shire. I shall be with him.' (ROTK, p. 267) Bilbo and [El]rond are here talking about that last journey. The ring Vilya, 'mightiest of [th]e Three', with its sapphire stone, can be seen on Elrond's hand.

The first part of Bilbo's journey with the dwarves was merry, but once they [ha]d left the Shire the weather turned cold and wet. They came across 'dreary [hi]lls, rising higher and higher, dark with trees. On some of them were castles [wi]th an evil look, as if they had been built by wicked people.' (H, p. 34)

'"Dawn take you all, and be stone to you!"' (H, p. 42) Tom, Bert and [W]illiam (Bill) Huggins – the trolls – had captured the dwarves and Bilbo.

Gandalf tricked them into arguing all night about the best way to cook their prisoners, until the sun rose and turned the trolls to stone. The trolls' cave where the swords Glamdring and Orcrist were discovered, and where Bilbo found the knife he later called *Sting*, is in the hill on the left.

4. 'With them went many Elves of the High Kindred who would no longer stay in Middle-earth.' (ROTK, p. 309) The elves who had decided to leave assemble at Rivendell. Galadriel is in the foreground on her white palfrey, with Bilbo on his grey pony.

i. The company with Elrond, when they rested at the Last Homely House for a while. The dwarves are (from the left): Ori (grey hood), Dwalin (dark green hood), Bifur (yellow hood), Gloin (white hood), Balin (red hood), Bofur (yellow hood, at the back), Fili (blue hood, fair hair), Bombur (pale green hood), Kili (blue hood, fair hair), Thorin Oakenshield (sky blue hood with a silver tassel, key on chain around neck), Oin (brown hood, at the back), Dori and Nori (purple hoods).

ii. 'One day they met a thunderstorm – more than a thunderstorm, a thunderbattle.' (H, p. 55)

5. 'Riding . . . behind on a small grey pony . . . was Bilbo himself.' (ROTK, p. 308) The ring Nenya, made of *mithril* with a white stone, can just be seen on Galadriel's hand.

i. 'Out jumped the goblins . . . and they were all grabbed.' (H, p. 58)

ii. 'Suddenly his hand met what felt like a tiny ring of cold metal lying on the floor of the tunnel.' (H, p. 65)

6. 22nd September 3021 (S.R. 1421): 'Frodo and Sam halted and sat silent in the soft shadows, until . . . the travellers came towards them.' (ROTK, p. 30) Frodo, riding Strider, and Sam, riding Bill, set out from Bag End on 21st September, and on the evening of 22nd joined the Last Riding of the Keepers of the Rings in Woody End. Frodo has a grey hood, Sam a red one.

i. 'Deep down here by the dark water lived old Gollum.' (H, p. 67)

ii. 'It was the trees at the bottom that saved them.' (H, p. 88) Having

...aped from the goblins, and come out on the eastern side of the Misty ...ountains, Bilbo and his friends are caught in a rock slide.

...Dawn, 29th September 3021 (S.R. 1421): 'They came to the Far Downs . . . ...d looked on the distant Sea.' (ROTK, p. 310)

..."*Fifteen birds in five firtrees*"' (H, p. 94) The Lord of the Eagles comes to the ...cue of the company: the flames from the goblins' fires can be seen in ...erse at the base of the trees. From the
...t, Fili and Kili have climbed a larch
...e, Dori, Nori, Ori, Oin, Gloin
...d Bilbo are in a pine, and Bifur,
...fur, Bombur and Thorin are in
...ther. Dwalin and Balin have
...en refuge in a fir tree, and
...ndalf is alone in a large pine tree.

..."Who are you and what do you want?"' (H, p. 105) Beorn the skin-
...anger talks with Gandalf and Bilbo. His bees (bigger than hornets) and
...hives are on the left, and his long low wooden house with two wings is in
...e background, with two of his horses.

'As they came to the gates, Círdan the Shipwright came forth to greet
...m.' (ROTK, p. 310) Gandalf is behind Círdan, wearing the Ring of Fire,
...rya the Great, with its red stone.

'The idea came to him to lead the furious spiders
...ther and further away from the dwarves.'
..., p. 138) It was in his first fight with
...e spiders of Mirkwood that Bilbo
...e his sword the name *Sting*. It
...s a blade made thousands of
...rs before in the hidden city of
...ndolin.

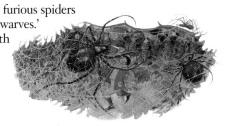

'Long and searchingly he questioned the dwarves
...ut their doings.' (H, p. 148) Thranduil, king of the Wood-elves, sits on his
...air of carven wood in his halls lit with red torch-light, and he is crowned
...h berries and red leaves. Thorin had been captured earlier, and was
...prisoned separately. Bilbo (invisible because he was wearing his ring) was
...ver caught.

9. 'Then Círdan led them to the Havens, and there was a white ship lying.' (ROTK, p. 310) Elrond, holding a silver harp, is standing behind the hobbi~

i. 'First he unlocked Balin's door.' (H, p. 154) Bilbo found being invisible enabled him to track down the cells in which each dwarf was imprisoned. ~ was visible when he rescued them: the dwarves had to see who he was and~ able to follow him.

ii. 'He found it quite as difficult to stick on as he had feared.' (H, p. 159) T~ picture is based on J.R.R. Tolkien's own colour painting of the barrels floating down the Forest River.

10. 'Up rode Merry and Pippin in great haste.' (ROTK, p. 310) Gandalf ha~ sent them a message, so that they could say farewell, and so that Sam shou~ not have to go home on his own.

i. 'They could see the Lonely Mountain towering grim and tall before ther~ (H, p. 173) As Bilbo and the dwarves journeyed towards the Lonely Mount~ (Mount Erebor) they stored some spare goods in a tent (extreme right of picture). The River Running rose out of the mountain and flowed out through the Front Gate.

ii. 'Stand by the grey stone when the thrush knocks, and the setting sun w~ the last light of Durin's Day will shine upon the key-hole.' (H, p. 52) The dwarves' New Year's Day was the first day of the last moon of Autumn on the threshold of Winter. When the moon and the sun were in the sky together it was called Durin's Day.

11. 'And the ship went out into the High Sea.' (ROTK, p. 310)

i. Bilbo, invisible because he is wearing the ring, steals a cup from Smaug's vast hoard – the dragon doesn't quite wake up. (H, pp. 184–5, 189)

ii. When Smaug attacked Esgaroth, he was fiercely resisted by archers led ~ Bard. Smaug's fiery breath set light to the thatched roofs, and many people including the Master, tried to escape in boats. Bard was told by the thrush of the one place – a hollow patch on the left breast – where Smaug was not armoured with jewels and gold embedded in his hide. (H, pp. 209–12)

. Evening, 29th September, 3021. The End of the Third Age. 'Sam . . . saw shadow on the waters that was soon lost in the West.' (ROTK, p. 311) The ing-bearers depart, and from this moment the Fourth Age is dated.

'The gate was blocked.' (H, p. 220) Faced by demands for compensation r damages from the men of Esgaroth, supported by their allies the Wood-ves, the dwarves fortified the Front Gate and altered the course of the eam to make a lake in front of it. Men and elves laid siege to the ountain.

. Attacked by goblins and wolves, the one-time foes – elves, men and varves – joined forces to fight the Battle of Five Armies. This picture ows the last phase of the battle, when the Eagles joined in.

5. '. . . white shores and beyond them a far green country under a swift unrise.' (ROTK, p. 310) The white ship has sailed beyond the bent seas of Iiddle-earth, and reached the Undying Lands.

'He would only take two small chests, one filled with silver, and the other ith gold, such as one strong pony could carry. "That will be quite as much I can manage," said he.' (H, p. 246) Bard would have rewarded Bilbo chly for all that he had done, but Bilbo would only accept a modest resent. After many months of adventures, he was glad to be heading home Gandalf's company.

. 'He was quite content.' (H, p. 254)